Breaking the Enemy Line

The Rise and Relief of Perry's Lake Erie Squadron

Jason Albers

Table of Contents

List of Illustrations

Preface

The entire idea to write this book was born to provide a simplified story about what led up to and after the Battle of Lake Erie. The decision was made overnight, but the lead-up took some time. Let's start from the beginning.

For a while, I had been discussing some of my projects with Matt, a friend also interested in history. We discussed various things, including the history of Plymouth, the Mayflower, and various topics related to the American Revolution around New England. When we started talking about the *USS Constitution*, he began to tell me about Luddam's Ford and the story of the anchors for the ship being forged there.

For those who do not know, Ludden's Ford Park in Hanover, Massachusetts, is the site of the former Curtis Anchor Forge. They made the anchors for the *Constitution* and a few other historic ships at some point.

A comment was made that they probably made all of the anchors for the Navy then, to which I responded with "*not for the ships that fought in the Great Lakes.*" Interestingly enough, just a day or so earlier, he had read about the Great Lakes battles and was curious about it. This led us to discuss the War of 1812, the Lake Erie Campaign, and Oliver Perry.

After a few days of history lessons (I make this as a joke because I said the same thing to him more than once), I made an off-the-collar comment about how it would be great if there were a movie or a television show about the Battle of Lake Erie. You see, what I haven't told you until now, the reader, is that Matt works in the film industry. So, he made some inquiries.

That brings us to the point of this book. It was suggested that a book or reference was used to form a screenplay. I looked around for a great book, but none had an excellent plot-style story. I then decided to go ahead and collect all the references and resources I could and assemble as authentic of a storyline for the Lake Erie Campaign as possible.

Along the way, I learned a few new things I had never known or didn't know the depth of and a few I had forgotten. For example, the history of the Navy Motto, Perry's flag at the battle, and the seven women who sewed it together for him. I was also unaware of the depth of the Perry-Elliott controversy, nor did I even know about Daniel Dobbins.

I believe Daniel Dobbins was left behind in history's account of the entire Lake Erie campaign. I genuinely think that the British would have won had it not been for the competence, knowledge, skill, and ingenuity of Dobbins. The U.S. leadership in the Great Lakes was so incompetent until the Dobbins-Perry team-up that I have little doubt that the United States could likely have reverted to a British colony or at least lost westward momentum in expansion.

My opinion, though, reflects on a what-if scenario, and I did say that I wanted to stay to an authentic version of history. So, I won't play that out in this book. Instead, I will quote a great author.

"Truth Is Stranger than Fiction, But It Is Because Fiction Is Obliged to Stick to Possibilities; Truth Isn't" – Mark Twain

Like Lord Byron, he acknowledges that the truth is a much more compelling and exciting story. I agree with them. History can move the world to great things when told with authenticity.

So here it is. I sincerely hope you all enjoy reading it as much as I did putting this all together.

Acknowledgments

I would not have gotten this book done without the guidance and assistance of the following people. They have been a source of inspiration and encouragement throughout this journey.

I first want to thank and recognize Matthew Scyber Wolo (Wolongevicz) for the many long discussions and for putting me on this path in the first place. This book would never have been a thought if it were not for him. If you are asking about that middle name, I learned recently that he got his name Scyber from the native word for 'Mountain Thunder Lion' before getting struck by lightning as if the name were an omen.

I also want to acknowledge the work of David Curtis Skaggs and Gerard T. Altoff. These two men have worked hard and diligently to research much about the Lake Erie campaign, Oliver Perry, Daniel Dobbins, and the actions around the Great Lakes during the War of 1812. They were a great source to begin my journey with.

After researching the Lake Erie campaign, I enjoyed spending time in Erie, Pennsylvania. Specifically, I was able to visit the Perry Monument on Presque Isle and the Erie Maritime Museum on the shores of Erie. I cannot express enough thanks and acknowledge for the help, guidance, and inspiration that the people of the Erie Maritime Museum were to me while I was there and since.

Finally, I thank my wife, Vanessa, for putting up with me and the crazy hours I spent working on this book. Without her support, there is no possible way I could have done it.

Introduction

There are undoubtedly hundreds of books about the life and times of Oliver Hazard Perry. He was an enigmatic figure in the War of 1812, the Barbary Wars, and other campaigns on the seas. Each author of those other books has their perspective about what he did at Lake Erie and how he pulled it off. From my perspective, he would not have gotten anywhere without a few others, and I will do my best to present that here.

Oliver Hazard Perry was born on August 13, 1785. It's almost cliché to start with a line like that, but in this case, it is essential to remember that date. For those who don't already know why, here is the spoiler: he dies on his birthday, not right away, but we'll get to that. He was born to Christopher Raymond Perry and his wife, Sarah Wallace Alexander. Oliver had a younger brother who was well known, too, Matthew Calbraith Perry.

Oliver's father, Christopher, was a decorated naval Captain of the American Revolutionary War. He started as a privateer aboard a few ships and was taken prisoner a couple of times. Each time, he escaped. I believe privateers were an example of naval excellence during the Revolution, but that is another discussion for another time. In 1799, Christopher arranged for his son Oliver to be commissioned as a Midshipman in the Navy and assigned to his ship, the *USS General Greene*. They cruised the Caribbean, escorting merchant ships to Cuba, before the ship settled for discharge in July 1800. Oliver was transferred to the *USS Adams* just as the first Barbary Wars began.

Oliver served with distinction for several years aboard the *Adams*, then the *Nautilus*. He eventually obtained positions onboard the *USS Constitution* and then the *USS Essex*. All of these experiences further aid in teaching him to be a good commander later.

In 1809, he was given command of the *USS Revenge*, whose mission was to patrol the seas and enforce the Embargo Act. This piece of legislation was passed by Congress in 1807 as an attempt by the United States to curtail the impressment of American sailors by the Royal Navy and protect American shipping from Britain and France during the Napoleonic Wars. Also, in 1809, Oliver's younger brother Mathew was given a warrant to the station of Midshipman and assigned to Oliver's ship, continuing the family legacy of naval service.

I will back up here and discuss some things that led to the War of 1812. A great deal of things happened in the decades before then. It can be argued that many of the following events contributed significantly to inciting the war to break out. I don't believe they happened in coincidence.

By February 1793, tensions between France and Great Britain got so high that France declared war against the island nation. The United States took a neutral position in the war, but Britain needed sailors. One of the issues was that in those days, as far as the British were concerned, the Americans were born as British subjects and, therefore, eligible to be pressed into service. They felt a person could not renounce their citizenship. The other issue was the harsh conditions of sea service and the high desertion rate. British sailors often heard of the better conditions and wages of American merchant shipping and jumped ship.

Thus, the Royal Navy would search American ships and take those sailors they found to be of the right age and fit to serve, often believing they may be British citizens since forged citizenship and merchant papers were easy to get. There was no international law to prevent it during the 18th century.

Another reason was the escalating trade tensions among France, Great Britain, and the United States. This led to significant measures such as the Embargo Act of 1807, which prohibited U.S. vessels from trading with European nations. Despite subsequent efforts like the Non-Intercourse Acts, aimed at resolving trade issues with France and Britain, tensions persisted. By 1810, attempts to reopen trade were made, contingent on halting blockades and impressment of American seamen. However, Britain's continued actions, which included stopping

American merchant ships and enforcing blockades, exacerbated tensions and trade disruptions.

The American people were angry. In the face of this, Former Chief Justice John Jay was appointed as a special envoy to help find a way to keep the peace. What resulted was a terrible agreement called the Jay Treaty that was unpopular but reluctantly passed by Congress. However, it slowed down tensions between the U.S. and Great Britain for a bit longer.

Another reason that tensions with Great Britain had remained high was the continued presence of British troops in the Northwest territory. At the end of the Revolutionary War, both parties signed the Treaty of Paris in 1783. One of the terms of this agreement was that the British would cede control of the territory to the United States and abandon the forts. They didn't. The soldiers continued to occupy the forts and support their indigenous allies in skirmishes against American settlers.

There had been an attempt by Congress to send military expeditions into the territory with the interest of settling unrest by the indigenous tribes and securing the lands for westward expansion. The results were not successful. It led to President Washington appointing a man by the name and title of General Anthony Wayne to the position of Commander of the Legion of the United States. This was a new professional Army. His mission was to clear out the tribes and make way for the settlers.

In August of 1794, he did so. At the Battle of Fallen Timbers, he led his troops to a considerable victory over the Confederation of Native Americans, assisted by his aide, William Henry Harrison. This confederation was led by Chief Little Turtle (of the Miami), Chief Blue Jacket (of the Shawnee), and Chief Buckongahelas (of the Lenape). The battle took place on the Maumee Rover near what is now Toledo, Ohio.

At that battle was a young Shawnee brave by the name of Tecumseh. He was a leader in Chief Bluejacket's forces but was defeated. Before and after this battle, he was a great orator; he later spent most of his time as a spokesman in the great councils.

Then, in 1804, the United States gained even more land through the Louisiana Purchase. This expanded westward beyond the Northwest Territory. As more settlers began passing through the land, the Indigenous tribes became more concerned, and in 1808, Tecumseh settled in present-day Indiana with his brother Tenskwatawa, "The Prophet. They devised a plan to abandon the white ways and form an Indian Confederation. Many tribes joined.

Several other things took place during the short time right before the War of 1812, and I believe they are interconnected to the War. However, it is in my mind that I think the events that I outlined here were of the greatest to note from this perspective. Tensions built up to the West of the building nation, and there were a few nefarious intentions by some members of the United States Congress that I will mention in a later chapter.

I believe that the inciting incident for the war was the heated attack between the Indigenous tribes and the overwhelming show of force by then-Governor William Henry Harrison at Tippecanoe in 1811. This battle resulted in the excuse that the war hawks in Congress needed to enact their plans for the northern border in Canada.

Prologue

The Battle of Tippecanoe

Tecumseh and his brother, Tenskwatawa, had been using Prophet's Town as a rallying point for recruits to their cause. The cause of a Confederacy of Indians that rejected the white man's way of life and returned to the old ways. Tenskwatawa had been seen as a holy man by many of these people, and as such, that is how the town got its name.

The United States Government at that time was very aggressive in its policy of expansion, specifically in seizing land from the indigenous tribes in the Northwest Territory and, later, the Louisiana Purchase. One of the chief 'negotiators' of the government in this expansion process was William Henry Harrison. He was ruthless and, in doing so, procured more than three million acres for white settlers from specifically selected tribes. This was one of the factors that led to his appointment as the Indiana territorial Governor.

Tecumseh had met with Governor Harrison at Vincennes in August of 1811 to insist that he and his brother only wanted peace. Meanwhile, he secretly accepted the British's aid in Canada, promising the Confederacy would join the British if hostilities broke out between Britain and the US. After the meeting with Tecumseh, Harrison also made a secret plan. He sent his secretary, John Gibson, to determine anything he could find out about the brothers. Gibson had learned about the gathering of native forces at Prophetstown. Harrison then gained permission and called up the militia along with the 4th U.S. Infantry via support from the Madison Administration to handle the Indian force.

On November 6, 1811, while Tecumseh was away on a recruiting mission to the south, Governor Harrison arrived at Prophetstown with more than one thousand troops. The Prophet sent out one of his followers with a white flag requesting a cease-fire and that the two leaders engage in a 'parley' before any action was taken. This would result in a delay since Tecumseh was not there. Harrison agreed to the terms and sent his forces a mile away to a hill on the banks of Burnett Creek.

According to stories and reports, the Governor was 'wary' of this ceasefire and arranged to have his men on standby. They were set up in a battle formation and were told to sleep with their weapons loaded. However, there was no order to build up fortifications. Was the Governor expecting something to happen?

According to further reports, that night, an African American wagon driver named Ben had defected from the American forces to the Shawnee. With the help of the defector, a plan was made to assassinate Harrison himself. Then Tenskwatawa was 'casting spells and speaking incantations' to protect his warriors in preparation for attack. However, the wagon driver was somehow recaptured while returning toward the American lines. The story goes that despite the failed assassination attempt, Tenskwatawa's forces did not withdraw but instead launched an attack. This took place at or around four in the morning on November 7th.

Interestingly, though it was very early in the morning, and without any warning, nearly all of the commands were almost instantly awake and ready to prepare commands. Shortly after this attack started, Captain Spencer of the Indiana Militia was struck and killed, quickly followed by his two Lieutenants. Apparently, Harrison was quickly alerted to the danger and somehow had the presence of mind to send two regular companies to support the camp's northern end.

War reports and other documentation go on to state that another attack happened at both the north and south ends of the camp but was successfully held. The Commander of the Daveiss Dragoons, Major Joseph Daveiss, was killed in action at the northern defense. The attacks lasted for over an hour.

Eventually, as the sun rose and 'revealed their inferior numbers,' the Native Americans retreated to Prophetstown. While this happened, Harrison fortified the camp, fearing they would return for another attack.

Back at Prophetstown, Tenskwatawa supposedly was confronted by the remainder of his forces about his 'magic not protecting them.' Unhappy with this, they abandoned him and left. Tenskwatawa himself also disappeared to the north into Canada.

The next day, on November 8th, Harrison sent a detachment into Prophetstown and found it abandoned except for a sick old woman. He ordered the town to be burned, all cooking implements to be burned, and anything else of value to be confiscated.

Some days after this happened, Tecumseh arrived back in Prophetstown, hearing a version of what had happened there. He decides to follow through with his promise to ally with the British and makes the journey north to Canada. This is the end of his dream of an Indian Confederacy.

Shawnee Chief Tecumseh. Courtesy of Toronto Public Library.

Declaration of War

After the events of Prophetstown, President Madison immediately summoned Congress into session. The pressure of the support by Britain for the Native Americans and the impressment of sailors on the high seas was reaching a boiling point. The American people were convinced that removing Britain from Canada would end the problems they were having with the indigenous tribes. At the same time, many Canadians believed that American expansionists were only using the Indian disputes as a pretext for engaging in a campaign of conquest.

Major General Isaac Brock, who led the British forces in Upper Canada during that period, didn't exactly ease the situation. Even though he was instructed to steer clear of escalating issues on the American frontier, settlers from the United States pointed fingers at British involvement in the increased tensions with Indians in the Northwest Territory. As the threat of war loomed, Brock aimed to bolster his regular and Canadian militia forces by forming alliances with Indian tribes, which intensified the concerns of American settlers.

Nevertheless, considerable discussions in Congress took place over the next few months. The Speaker of the House was a War Hawk from Kentucky named Henry Clay. He and his fellow Expansionists advocated heavily for war with Canada. Looking back on his life and career, it is unknown if he genuinely favored the war or if it was the best political deal he saw because history records him as "The Great Compromiser." According to all accounts, he could ignore his principles. His ultimate loyalty was to what he felt was the 'health of the union.'

Things came to a head on June 1, 1812, when President Madison sent a message of War to Congress. Congress voted. The House of Representatives voted in favor of 79-49, while the Senate echoed this sentiment with a 19-13 vote. The divide primarily surfaced between seafaring New England states, which opposed the war, and Southern and Western states, which supported it. Federalists accused war advocates of expansionism disguised as protecting American maritime rights. However, the primary motive was not expansionism but the determination to defend American honor. The United States attacked Canada because it was under British control, but there was no widespread ambition to annex the region.

Acquiring East and West Florida from Spain motivated Southern backing for the war, yet Southerners and Westerners were concerned about the United States' global reputation. Additionally, British trade restrictions negatively impacted American farmers by preventing the export of their produce to Europe. Even regions seemingly detached from maritime issues had a vested interest in safeguarding neutral shipping. For those Americans, "Free trade and sailors' rights" held genuine significance.

President Madison signed the declaration of war on June 18, 1812.

Ironically, two days earlier, the British government had repealed the 1807 Orders in Council, two of the leading causes of the war. The British Orders in Council limited American trade with Europe and decreed impressment of sailors, the Royal Navy's practice of taking seamen from American merchant vessels to augment their critically undermanned crews aboard their warships.

GROUNDING OF THE USS REVENGE

Earlier in 1811, on the 9th of January, the *USS Revenge* ran aground with Lieutenant Oliver Perry in command. This took place just off the coast of Rhode Island, and the ship was ultimately lost at sea. Accordingly, Lieutenant Perry took swift action to get his crew off safely and was the last to leave the ship. After an investigation, they blamed the ship's pilot for the incident but gave Perry a leave of absence. During this time, he married the love of his life, Elizabeth Champlin Mason, on May 5th, 1811. They enjoyed an extended honeymoon around the New England states.

It is essential to know the context and location of where Oliver Perry was and what he was doing during 1811 and 1812, as he will play a significant part in the events.

In June 1812, after the war was declared, Perry received orders to command gunboat construction in Newport, Rhode Island. He immediately began petitioning his superiors for a better assignment directly in the war.

Commodore Oliver H. Perry.
Courtesy of Toronto Museum of Art.

Midshipman Turner

Captain Daniel Turner. Courtesy of USS Constitution Museum.

A young native of New York named Daniel Turner, having previously served on the *USS Constitution* and then transferred to the frigate President, was given his first command at the onset of the war.

In June 1812, Midshipman Turner was ordered to Norwich, Connecticut, to command the gunboat squadron there. He had only been a warranted Midshipman for four years, but he, too, will make an essential contribution later in this story and the war.

The Invasion Of Canada

At that time, the British were still very much preoccupied with the Napoleonic War. This led American government officials to feel overly confident that their war in the North was going to be over quickly. However, the United States was just as ill-prepared for war as the British in Canada. They didn't know it at the time.

The Secretary of War, William Eustis, infamously claimed that the Americans could take Canada without soldiers, needing only officers, and that the Canadian people would rally to the American standard. Henry Clay believed that the Kentucky militia alone would be able to defeat and occupy Montreal and Upper Canada.

They were not the only ones to make bold claims and statements. Thomas Jefferson wrote on August 4, 1812:

"The acquisition of Canada this year, as far as the neighborhood of Quebec, will be a mere matter of marching, and will give us

experience for the attack of Halifax the next, and the final expulsion of England from the American continent."

They were all proved wrong.

On July 12, Hull led an invasion into Upper Canada. While planning an attack on the British at Fort Amherstburg, a small British force strategically surrounded the U.S. garrison at Fort Mackinac, taking the Americans by surprise and leading to a swift surrender. Despite this, Hull faced challenges in assaulting the well-defended British positions and safeguarding a stretched supply line as far as Ohio. Faced with a stalemate, Hull returned to Detroit in early August.

Boosted by their recent victory at Fort Mackinac and Hull's withdrawal, the British forces geared up for an offensive. A few days later, Tecumseh, with the support of British Regulars, defeated a force sent by Hull to open his supply line at Monguagon, north of Frenchtown. Brock took advantage of Hull's psychological state with the momentum in their favor. On August 15, Brock informed the American commander that he wouldn't be able to control Tecumseh's warriors if he didn't surrender. The next day, Brock surrounded Detroit. Fearful of being attacked by the native forces, Hull surrendered without firing a single shot, an act seen by many on both sides as disgraceful.

Section 1

Section I

The Capture of Fort Mackinac

Before the War of 1812, the Great Lakes region thrived on the trade of salt and furs, with salt being the prized commodity crucial for preserving fish and meats without refrigeration. For example, In 1811 alone, Captain Daniel Dobbins and his crew transported over $120,000 worth of salt aboard his schooner *Salina* from Mackinaw, Michigan.

However, the peaceful trade atmosphere was disrupted when British forces raided Fort Mackinac on July 17, 1812, capturing Captain Dobbins and his partners, Rufus S. Reed and William W. Reed.

At the time, no one except the British knew about the declaration of war between the United States and Britain. The trio were offered parole under the condition that they wouldn't "take up arms against the United Kingdom."

Resolute and independent, Dobbins, the Reeds, and their crew resisted pledging allegiance to the crown or promising not to take arms against the British.

During this time, a wealthy American fur trader named John Jacob Aster had heard about the war declaration and sent out riders westward to warn his trading outposts. Often, the British intercepted his messages before they could reach any Americans.

Daniel Dobbins. Courtesy of Buffalo and Erie County Historical Society.

At Mackinac, a deadlock ensued between Dobbins and the crew of the *Salina* and the British until Mr. Wilmoth of the British Northwest Fur Company intervened, negotiating a deal to allow the *Salina* to leave port as a cartel ship bound for Fort Malden in Amherstburg, Canada. The following day, the ship and crew set sail towards Detroit and Fort Malden.

Despite the British directive to sail to Fort Malden, Dobbins chose a different path, meeting General William Hull at Fort Detroit.

Brock Joins the Fight

British Major General Isaac Brock was in York when Mackinac was captured dealing with the provincial government matters. However, with more British forces sent to the lines, Brock left York on August 5th, interrupting the government assembly. He and his forces arrived at Amherstburg on 13 August at the same time as Tecumseh and his forces arrived. On arrival, Brock received the captured dispatches for General Hull onboard the *Cuyahoga* headed to Detroit from Ohio and the additional documents captured at Brownstown.

Brock learned from Hull's dispatches that his force's morale was low and that they feared the number of Indians that they might be facing. Brock used this information to his advantage and arranged for a false letter to fall into American hands at Detroit for Hull to appear as if there were five thousand Indians already at Amherstburg and heading for Detroit. Although Brock only had nearly 600 warriors.

On August 15, Brock sent a letter to Hull after he was sure the American General had seen the false letter demanding his surrender. The fear alone got to Hull.

The Surrender of Detroit

Instead of sailing to Fort Malden as ordered by the British, Dobbins met up with General William Hull at Fort Detroit, arriving on the third of August. While the *Salina* and Dobbins were there, a British force under the command of General Isaac Brock, with the support of Tecumseh and his men, surrounded the Fort. Captain Dobbins and his crew were again taken prisoner when General Hull surrendered Detroit to the British a couple of days later, on August 16, 1812.

At some point, Dobbins's captors figured out that he broke his alleged promise of "not taking up arms against the British" by taking part in the defense of Detroit. Fortunately for Dobbins, before he could be executed, a friend of his from before the war, British Colonel Robert Nichols, helped him to escape and granted him safe passage to Cleveland, Ohio, where he eventually found and reported what happened to General David Meade. However, the British kept his ship as a supply ship this time.

USS Adams. Courtesy of Toronto Public Library.

At the time of Hull's surrender, Detroit had the only American naval ship on the entire Great Lakes, the *USS Adams*. Upon Hull's surrender, the British commandeered and renamed the brig HMS Detroit.

Madison's Concerns for the Great Lakes

General Meade sent Captain Dobbins to Washington with the news. While in Washington in September 1812, Daniel Dobbins was invited by the Secretary of Navy, Paul Hamilton, to a conference regarding Lake Erie. Upon his arrival, Dobbins discovered that Hamilton wanted the benefit of his knowledge and experience on the Great Lakes. He asked for his input on the best location for constructing an American fleet of warships on Lake Erie.

For approximately ten days, President Madison and his Cabinet deliberated on the vulnerable state of the American side of Lake Erie. They and the President recognized the need for warships and the importance of building them at Lake Erie. When asked, Dobbins, without hesitation, proposed Presque Isle as the ideal location due to its sheltered harbor, offering protection during construction and potential battles with the British.

He further highlighted the abundance of oak, ash, and chestnut trees in the area, along with cedar trees on Presque Isle, a source that he felt was desirable for various parts of the ships. These factors made Erie a highly favorable location for ship construction.

Before departing Washington, acting on Madison's directive, Hamilton appointed Dobbins as a Sailing Master in the U.S. Navy. Accompanied by a letter of instruction, Dobbins was tasked with promptly proceeding to Presque Isle to secure the necessary timber and supplies for building a minimum of four gunboats. Hamilton also gave him sketches and dimensions of the four gunboats to be constructed at Erie.

Command of the Great Lakes

A few days before Dobbins was ordered to build the fleet at Washington, on September 12, Captain Isaac Chauncey was ordered to Sacketts Harbor at the east end of Lake Huron to take command and gain control of the Great Lakes. Dobbins was sent to report to him on his way to Erie and keep him advised on the progress of the ship construction. At the same time that Chauncey was ordered to Sacketts Harbor, his second in command, Lieutenant Jesse D. Elliott, also received orders.

At Sacketts Harbor, a few small merchant ships were based in York, now called Toronto. After checking in with Captain Chauncey, Sailing Master Dobbins returned to Erie and began working, employing Ebenezer Crosby as his Master Shipwright and sending word to the Captain per his instruction. Failing to hear word back, Dobbins traveled to Black Rock and only met with Chauncey's aid Lieutenant Angus.

Shortly after visiting Lt Angus, Dobbins received word from Elliott by letter, which appeared to ignore Dobbins' authorization from the Secretary of the Navy. In the letter were the words:

> *"It appears to me utterly impossible to build gunboats at Presque Isle .... You shall again hear from me."*

Elliott took it upon himself to begin converting five merchant ships into a naval squadron at Black Rock for Lake Erie operations. Dobbins, of course, responded:

> *"I believe I have as perfect a knowledge of this lake as any other man on it, and I believe this is the place [Erie] for a naval station."*

The Ships of Black Rock

On October 9, 1812, *Caledonia* and *HMS Detroit* (formerly the American armed brig *Adams* captured at the Siege of Detroit) were anchored near Fort Erie in the upper reaches of the Niagara River. Both had transported troops and materials eastwards, with *Caledonia* also carrying a valuable cargo of furs.

A joint American expedition, led by Lieutenant Jesse Elliott and Army Captain Nathan Towson, seized the two brigs. *Caledonia* was taken to the Navy Yard at Black Rock, becoming the *USS Caledonia*. However, the current swept *Detroit* away, and it had to drop anchor within range of British cannons.

Elliott engaged in battle with the shore emplacement until he ran out of ammunition. He then beached the ship on Squaw Island (what is now called Unity Island) and escaped to the American side of the river. The beached ship was then destroyed by gunfire from both British and American cannons.

At Black Rock, the schooners Somers, Amelia, and Ohio, along with the sloop Trippe, all purchased by the United States Navy and undergoing conversion into gunboats, were also present. Due to the British control of Fort Erie and nearby batteries dominating the Niagara River, these vessels were effectively pinned down and unable to leave Black Rock.

Lieutenant Jesse Elliott. Courtesy of New York Public Library.

Unfortunately, *Detroit* had been destroyed. It may have been an additional ship that Lieutenant Elliot attempted to procure for the Erie Squadron.

Construction of the Erie Fleet

Dobbins and Crosby continued their work under the orders they were given. They never faltered in their or hesitated. For weeks, no word came from Chauncey or Elliott, and they even visited Black Rock with no success. Finally, he relented and sent word of the situation to the Secretary of the Navy in Washington on December 12, 1812, asking for help and more money.

The letter had achieved its desired effect, and on New Year's Eve 1812, Chauncey and a renowned shipbuilder, Henry Eckford, arrived in Erie. While they were there, Eckford made several alterations to the designs of the gunboats to maximize survivability while sailing on the Lakes. The order was also increased to include two additional brigs. These brigs were to be outfitted with 37 total 32-pound carronade guns.

The next day, on New Year's Day, both men left Erie and never returned. However, upon arrival at Black Rock, Captain Chauncey requested the Secretary of the Navy to order Oliver H. Perry to Erie to command the Erie squadron.

Word also got sent that a Master Shipwright named Noah Brown from New York would join them to assist in construction.

Ghost Ship on the Erie

That December, Dobbins and his construction crew desperately needed materials to equip their partially built gunboats at Erie. In an unexpected turn of events, a "ghost" ship emerged offshore, trapped in winter's icy grip. Seizing the opportunity, Dobbins orchestrated a salvage operation, hauling sleds over the frozen expanse.

To Dobbins' astonishment, the ship trapped in the ice was none other than his former ship, the *Salina*. Earlier in December, the ship had got caught in the Lake Erie ice, and the British crew had abandoned it.

This fortuitous discovery proved invaluable as Dobbins decided to remove everything he could use. Everything that could be reused from the *Salina* was taken or converted for the ships that would become part of Perry's fleet.

Section 2

New Leadership in Washington

With the significant losses from General Hull's surrender at Detroit, Secretary of War William Eustis was heavily criticized. Many had felt he never should have been in the position in the first place, having no qualifications to be there. Despite minor attempts to improve military readiness before the war, he ultimately knew there was no way out and resigned in December 1812. Secretary of State James Monroe filled in until John Armstrong was selected and took the helm.

John Armstrong immediately set out to make valuable changes in the military forces that contributed to the Armed Forces' success. However, he adamantly believed that the British would never attack Washington DC and did nothing to prepare for its defense.

One of his changes was to promote Oliver Hazard Perry to the rank of Commodore and give him orders to take charge at Erie. Perry was also given the authority to take 150 men (Some of them from the *USS Constitution*) and his younger brother, Alexander. Perry and his crew left Rhode Island on February 22, 1813.

Perry Arrives in Sacketts Harbor

It took nine days for Perry's crew to arrive at Sacketts Harbor instead due to the heavy weather. When they arrived, Perry reported to Captain Chauncey to determine the situation he was facing. Instead, Chauncey retained Perry and his crew for two weeks to wait for a possible threat of attack by the British from Kingston.

A few weeks earlier, on February 10th, plans were drawn up for the Americans to attack Kingston and York before capturing Fort George. While the first assault happened, another American force would capture Fort Erie and meet up with the first to take Fort George. The problem was that the Americans received false information that a British force of 6000-8000 men was preparing for an attack on Sacketts Harbor.

Two weeks later, when the attack never happened, Chauncey kept Perry's men that he brought with him but ordered him to Erie to get the construction back on track.

Perry Goes to Erie

Due to the harsh winter conditions, Perry and his brother endured an eleven-day journey to Erie, finally arriving on March 26. After they arrived, Dobbins informed Perry of the vulnerable state of the ships and the town. Recognizing the imminent and potential danger, Perry sent word to General Meade to set up a meeting about the town's security and shipyards.

That meeting with Meade resulted in one thousand militia being housed at Garrison Hill, which additional volunteers gradually reinforced.

On the Canadian shore of Lake Erie, it was believed that most citizens were British sympathizers who had relocated after the Revolutionary War. As effective spies, they provided the British with intelligence on Perry's movements and the progress of ship construction.

Blockhouses were strategically constructed and manned near each shipyard and the harbor entrance to counter these potential threats. The militia provided constant guards to prevent enemy spies or actors from sabotaging the ship workers or accessing the town.

Construction Continues

After the town and shipyards at Erie were safe, Perry took the next step to get the work back on track. He left for Pittsburgh on 31 March to sign a contract for much-needed supplies. This was the first of several trips over the next few months. He also retained the services of George Foxall of Washington, DC, to create the 37 carronades and have them delivered to Erie, along with the additional ones already sent to Sacketts Harbor.

His trips resulted in 150 carpenters hired from New York and many block-makers, sailmakers, and riggers from Philadelphia. The work was getting done quickly. Another Master Shipwright hired by Washington, named Noah Brown, also arrived.

Work had progressed so well that in the middle of April, the ships *Tigress* and *Porcupine* were launched from the Lee's Run yard. The *Scorpion* was expected to be completed within weeks. Perry needed his men to crew these ships, so he requested them from Captain Chauncey. After not getting a satisfactory answer, he traveled to Sacketts Harbor to make his request again in person.

Battle of York

Perry had arrived at Sacketts Harbor shortly before 23 April. Plans had been drawn up for an attack on York and now were ready to be implemented. Captain Chauncey had ordered Perry to participate in this skirmish in command of the twelve Schooners. Also joining this battle was Brigadier General Zebulon Pike, leading the 1st Rifle Regiment, several US Infantry units, and the 3rd Artillery. Major General Henry Dearborn and Commodore Chauncey were overall commanders onboard the *USS Madison* (A corvette sloop built at Sacketts Harbor only a few months earlier) to oversee, with Lieutenant Elliot in command of Chauncey's ship.

The assault was delayed on the day until 24 April; the British were not prepared. On the 27th, the first landing force of soldiers, the 1st Rifle Regiment, began arriving and immediately engaged enemy forces. Perry, meanwhile, has been successfully destroying shore artillery guns and defenses, as the gunboats were assisting the assault force using grapeshot and heavy shot.

The British troops led by Major General Roger Sheaffe quickly realized he was outmanned and outgunned. He ordered a retreat and set fire to the bridge over the River Don, leaving the militia and several citizens behind. He instructed those left behind to set fire to the ship at the dock and to blow up the fort's magazine.

The magazine had been successfully rigged for the explosion but was not completed. General Pike and several of his troops were near the magazine questioning a prisoner during the bombarding by Chauncey's squadron when it was struck, causing it to ignite. The explosion killed Pike and 37 American soldiers and drove the remaining American forces to retreat to safety.

The American attack on York in 1813. Courtesy of the Public Archives of Canada.

The British forces did not attempt to recapture the fort; instead, Captain John Robinson of the York Militia was the officer who negotiated with the Americans for the official surrender of York.

Over the next few days, the American forces looted and destroyed important sites at York in defiance of orders by Generals Pike and Dearborn.

The Burning of York

The city of York became a battleground during the War of 1812 as American troops descended upon it in the aftermath between April 28 and 30. The first building of the Legislative Assembly and several others were set ablaze. Before departing from York, the Americans razed much of the fort's structures, leaving destruction in their wake. What ensued was not just a military conflict but a wave of plunder and destruction.

American soldiers, during their occupation, unleashed havoc upon the city. Acts of looting were rampant, and some troops took it upon themselves to set fire to significant structures, including the Legislative Assembly and Government House, the residence of the Lieutenant Governor of Upper Canada. They claimed that they had discovered a 'scalp,' later revealed to be the Speaker's wig, as the reason for the act of wanton vandalism.

The Printing Office, a hub for official documents and newspapers, had also fallen victim to vandalism, with the printing press mercilessly smashed. Empty houses even became targets, with American soldiers looting them under the pretext that the absent owners were militia members who had not been given their required parole. Even the homes of Canadians associated with the Natives were not spared from the looting spree.

During the chaos, Chauncey's officers took books from York's first subscription library. When Chauncey found out, he was embarrassed and attempted to return the books during the second incursion in July. Unfortunately, the library had already closed, and the books were eventually auctioned in 1822.

The Burning of Newark. Courtesy of U.S. National Park Service

The soldiers ignored orders not to loot civilian property, going against earlier commands from Generals Pike and Dearborn. Dearborn, embarrassed by his troops' actions, either couldn't or would not control or stop them. This disregard for orders and protests from local leaders made the American General eager to leave York once they transported the captured goods. The Burning of York had a lasting impact on the city, its buildings, and relations between the warring factions. It was even said to contribute to the burning of Washington, D.C., later in the war.

New British Commander of Erie Naval Squadron

Captain Robert Barclay. Courtesy of Windsor Public Library, Ontario.

Following the outbreak of war with America, Admiral Sir John Borlase Warren, 1st Baronet, Commander in Chief on the North American station, assigned Captain Robert Barclay and two other lieutenants, Robert Finnis and Daniel Pring, as "Captains of Corvettes" on the Great Lakes. Barclay assumed command of the squadron in Kingston on Lake Ontario on May 5, 1813, with the acting rank of Commander. However, just ten days later, he was replaced by Captain James Lucas Yeo.

Yeo then initially offered the command of Lake Erie to William Mulcaster, who declined due to the undermanned and underequipped state of the force. The position was then offered to Barclay, who promptly accepted.

At the time, the Americans dominated Lake Ontario and the Niagara Peninsula, compelling Barclay to travel overland to Amherstburg, accompanied by a small group of officers and seamen, the base of his new command.

Battle of Fort George

After the events at York, the American forces were taken by ship to Fort Niagara, where they stayed for a few weeks to recover and prepare for the next leg of the short campaign.

Brigadier General John Vincent led the British forces at Fort George, comprising 1,000 regular soldiers and 300 militia, including Captain

Runchey's Company of Coloured Men. Anticipating an imminent assault, Vincent strategically divided his regulars into three detachments to counterattack the Americans.

However, the unexpected occurred on May 27, as an early morning fog lifted, revealing American vessels off the lake shore to the west. The attack did not follow the anticipated route along the Niagara River. Major Benjamin Forsyth led the U.S. 1st Rifle Regiment, two companies of the U.S. 15th Infantry, and the bulk of the U.S. 2nd Artillery, fighting as infantry. The Glengarry Light Infantry and the Royal Newfoundland engaged fiercely, resulting in casualties.

As the battle unfolded, British troops counterattacked Winfield Scott's forces, reinforced by the remnants of earlier engagements. Perry's schooners played a significant role, causing heavy losses among the British. With the arrival of Boyd's brigade, Vincent realized he was outnumbered and outflanked, opting to retreat south to Queenstown.

Despite Vincent's order to spike guns and destroy the fort's magazines, the retreat was swift, allowing the Americans to keep the fort intact. A close pursuit by Scott and bombardment from American batteries across the river added pressure on the retreating British. Scott's forces resisted rearguards, including Merritt's Troop of Provincial Dragoons.

The American plan, however, included Colonel James Burn's dragoons crossing the Niagara and cutting off Vincent's retreat. Although delayed by a British battery, Burn strategically waited for reinforcements before attempting to move against Vincent. However, fearing an ambush, Major General Lewis ordered Scott to abandon the pursuit. They had already won.

The Ships of Black Rock

After American forces successfully captured the British forts along the Niagara River, Perry could take the rest of his squadron's ships from

Black Rock to Erie. Commodore Chauncey recognized that Perry's fleet would need manning and finally assigned him 65 men for those ships.

Unfortunately, it would not be easy since the ships were upriver in the Niagara River, so Perry had to obtain an oxen team to pull them against the current into the open of Lake Erie. With 250 soldiers and sailors, the crew and team took six days to complete the grueling task.

To make matters worse, the ships were all but unarmed, and they would have to sail them back to Erie, knowing that there might be a British force on the water waiting for them.

Barcley Sails from Amherstburg

On about 5 June, Barclay arrived in Amherstburg. Eager to get to work and under the belief and understanding that the Americans had no armed ships on the Lake, he set sail aboard his ship, the *Queen Charlotte*, with what little crew he had.

His first stop was to reconnoiter the shipyard at Presque Isle. His first surprise was the sandbar that prevented an attempt to achieve a naval assault to destroy the ships in the bay. He next asked for help for a land assault from Major General Francis de Rottenburg, who refused because the military forces there were well-defended. Things were not looking well as he discovered that Perry also had superior numbers in ships, although he was unsure if Perry had the seamen to man them.

Not finding a solution to stop the Americans at Erie, he set sail toward Black Rock, having also heard of the ships there. He believed they would be moved to Presque Isle and wanted to intercept them.

Black Rock Fleet Sails to Presque Isle

Shortly after the ships made it out onto the open lake, the weather became unfavorable, and a headwind from the east struck up, making it very hard for the ships to sail to Erie. At about the same time, they spotted sails out on the horizon in the direction they needed to go: the *Queen Charlotte*.

Before the British can spot them or even get to an intercept point, fog rolls in, and the American fleet can slip by. This doesn't deter Barclay as he attempts to pursue through the fog and the nights. The ships came within miles of each other for the next three days.

Miraculously, the Americans can get ahead of Barclay to Erie and safely slip over the sand bar into port without notice. After the fog lifts, Barclay finds the fleet at Presque Isle and sets up a blockade to prevent Perry's fleet from leaving the harbor.

Upon Perry's arrival, he was relieved that the *Scorpion* had been completed, and both brigs, yet to be named, were getting their final touches. The final ship, a pilot boat named *Ariel,* also nearing completion, was receiving its sails and decking.

Section 3

Don't Give up the Ship!

On June 1, the *USS Chesapeake* sailed out of Boston Harbor and was quickly met by *HMS Shannon*. The captain of the *Shannon*, Captain Philip Broke, had issued a written challenge to the Chesapeake days earlier, but it was not delivered before the ship undocked.

The two ships immediately engaged in battle, but the Chesapeake had a challenge. The ship's wheel and part of the rigging were destroyed in the initial blows, making the ship maneuverable. To add to the list of challenges, Captain James Lawrence, who had only taken command of the ship ten days earlier, was killed in the volley. His last command to his crew was to "don't give up the ship," an order they could not comply with.

The battle lasted less than fifteen minutes and resulted in 252 sailors being killed or wounded, including the *Shannon's* Captain as well. The senior surviving officer of the British ship took the American ship and crew back to Nova Scotia, where they were imprisoned, and the ship was repaired and pressed into the Royal Navy.

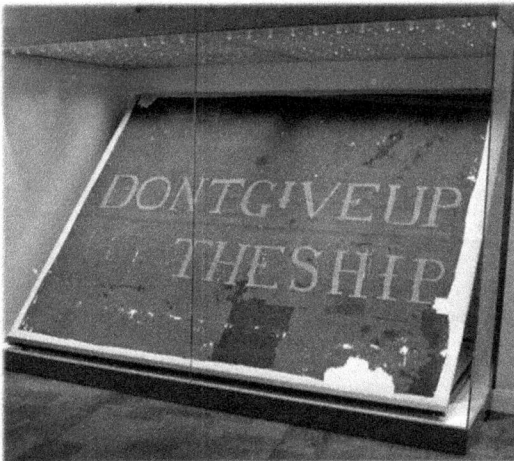

Perry's Flag. Courtesy of U.S. Navy Academy.

Barclay's Blockade

For weeks, Barclay and his small fleet of six ships sat outside of Presque Isle, taunting Perry for action. The two commanders were itching for the sea battle of the ages. Perry, having only 120 sailors, did not have the manpower to get his ships across the bar to fight. By his account, he needed about 740 to get underway and give the British the fight they deserved.

During this blockade, the shipwrights checked over the ships from Black Rock and worked on upgrades and outfitting. They had also determined that the Amelia would be unfit for service as a combat ship and left at the docks. Perry also assigned all the ships a Captain except for the other brig, leaving that for a senior officer he expected to receive from Commodore Chauncey.

At the same time, he received letters from the Secretary of the Navy and other local Generals urging him to get his fleet into the fight. He was needed at Fort Meigs, to which he could only respond with his regrets that his forces were not yet ready for service.

In mid-July, as the final ship was complete, he received word that one of his closest friends, James Lawrence, had been killed in the line of duty. In Perry's frustration, he urged Commodore Chauncey to send men repeatedly. He also asked the sailmakers to create a flag with the line that his friend uttered as his last command, "Don't give up the ship," and christened his flagship, the *Lawrence*. He also named the other brig *Niagara*.

The letter writing and frustration intensified from Perry to his commander with Barclay just outside the harbor. He even suggested the Commodore come to Erie and take charge in his 23 July letter. In that letter to Chauncey, he vehemently wrote, '*Send me men and officers ... send on the commander, my dear sir, for the Niagara. She is a noble vessel ... send me officers and men, and honour is within our grasp.*'

Reinforcements for the Fleet

A few days after Perry had sent the letter to Commodore Chauncey, a welcome surprise arrived at Erie. Perry's cousin, Stephen Champlin, had marched into town with seventy men, primarily African American and other militiamen. Champlin had been given the rank of Sailing Master and assigned to Perry by his superior officers in Sacketts Harbor. Perry gave him command of the *Scorpion.*

A week later, another sixty men arrived from Sacketts Harbor for the fleet. Most were too sick to stand; some trembled with 'lake fever.' Perry even tried to recruit from Meade's militia forces assigned to Erie. Not more than a handful signed on.

There was little else he could do but wait. He requested the militia to stand watch onboard the ships for worry that the British would send armed men in small boats to destroy them. The militia refused, a common problem during the war and why the Regular Army and Navy despised militia.

Niagara's Captain

Meanwhile, on 27 July, Commodore Chauncey promoted Jesse Elliott to Master Commandant and assigned him as second in charge of Perry's squadron. Elliott saw this as an insult as he felt that Perry was his lesser; whether that was due to a lack of knowledge of who Perry was or arrogance on Elliott's part, is a separate debate. Nonetheless, Elliot felt that Perry lacked sufficient combat experience and was already vocal in his critical opinions of Presque Isle as a shipyard.

Perry had informed Chauncey that he needed a Captain for the *Niagara,* and the Commodore informed Elliott of the position. He sent him and eighty-nine other men to Presque Isle to report to Perry for service.

Barclay's Dinner Party

Perry's luck kicked in once more. On the night of 31 July, the British fleet outside of Presque Isle had disappeared. There were no lights from the ships. Nothing. An aide immediately woke Perry with the news, and Perry went to the shore to see and search for himself. After a bit, Perry recalled a report he received about a dinner in Barclay's honor at Port Dover. The Commander had accepted. This was good news for the American fleet.

Barclay believed that the Americans would never be able to get their ships across the shallow bar and even further thought that they would try and get stuck. Historically, we found out that he told the audience at his dinner party that he expected to find them at the bar and make a small job of destroying them when he returned.

Sending the Fleet Over The Bar

Barclay was at least partly correct. Perry immediately decided to get the fleet across the bar. At around 4 a.m. on 1 August, the schooners and gunboats were at the mouth of the harbor waiting while Daniel Dobbins sounded the bar. The brigs got in line as well, *Lawrence* first, then *Niagara*.

It was clear that the brigs would have a hard time, but another miracle happened, and shipwright Sidney Wright had constructed gadgets called camels. They were essentially submersible pontoons designed to lift the brigs over the bar. At first, they worked, but it was not enough, and the ship had to remove some weight. Perry ordered the removal of the cannons and stores. Even with the eventual help of the Pennsylvania Militiamen, it took three days to get *Lawrence* over the bar.

Cameling the Brigs. Courtesy of Erie Maritime Museum blog.

Immediately as soon as the ship slid into deep water, the cannons and stores were quickly put back on, and the crews readied the *Niagara* for its turn across the bar. On 5 August, Niagara stuck on the bar and was about to be fitted for the camels when sails were spotted on the horizon.

Barclay had returned from his dinner party. Had the Commander been correct in his prediction? Just as the British fleet was coming closer to range, the winds shifted to the west, causing the noses of the American brigs to swing in the British direction. Barclay believed that Perry was coming to fight. Had Barclay misjudged the depth of the water at the bar?

First Shots on the Erie

Perry immediately recognized the chance at a bluff and took it. He ordered his men to man the *Lawrence* and called for his drummer to beat to quarters. The men jumped aboard, readied up, and were at their stations.

He then sent out the *Ariel* and *Scorpion* to attack the enemy fleet with their long guns, to which they sent a couple of volleys.

What Perry didn't know, was that Barcley was as severely undermanned as he was. He signaled his captains to turn their helms over and retreat to open water. The two American ships gave a small chase for a moment, long enough to keep up the deception.

For this short cruise, the following officers and ships were involved: *Lawrence* - Commodore Perry; *Niagara* - Lieutenant Daniel Turner; *Caledonia* - Purser Humphrey Magrath; *Ariel* - Lieutenant John Packet; *Scorpion* - Sailing Master Stephen Champlin; *Somers* - Sailing Master Thomas Almy; *Tigress* - Master's Mate A. McDonald; *Porcupine* - Midshipman George Senat. *Ohio* and *Trippe* were left at the docks due to a lack of crew.

The Lawrence also sailed out for about a day to search for the British but did not find them and returned to Presque Isle as the remaining crews were all working on getting the *Niagara* over the bar. Perry discharged some of the militia who had ridden along and then turned to work on the *Niagara*. At dinner on 6 August, he received news that Jesse Elliott and some reinforcements would arrive soon. Perry sent the *Ariel* down the shoreline to meet them and bring them sooner.

Jesse Elliott Takes Command of Niagara

Elliott was less than friendly toward Perry and his senior staff when he arrived. While Perry greeted him and spoke highly of his love of country and military glory, Elliott all but scoffed at him. Even Perry's sailing master, William Taylor, tried to warn Perry that Elliott was not his friend, but Perry did not care. Every man was a blessing that he needed and ignored the breaches of courtesy that Elliott was performing toward his superior.

Out of the 89 men that Elliott brought with him, he chose the best of them for himself on the *Niagara*. According to the record, he arrived with his officers as well which were two Lieutenants, eight midshipmen, and a master's mate.

The British Retreat to Malden

After the British sailed across the open waters, Barclay determined it was time to set course for Fort Malden. Having commissioned the construction of a new ship earlier, he signaled his fleet to make their way swiftly. Upon reaching Malden, they were greeted by an impressive 19-gun brig anchored in the port – the vessel Barclay had eagerly awaited.

Impressed by this ship, he named it *Detroit*, in homage to the victorious encounter the British had against Hull, and proudly declared it his new flagship.

Setting Sail for Put-In-Bay

Perry had made his way to meet with General William Harrison. They liked each other from the beginning. They discussed a location for the fleet to set at anchor to wait for the British fleet and fresh supplies. Harrison suggested South Bass Island at Put-in-Bay, and Perry agreed. Perry then returned to Erie to get the fleet underway.

On 12 August, all the ships were over the bar, and all the men were assigned; the ships were ready to go, and the fleet set sail for Put-in-Bay.

The command assignments were set as follows:

- *Lawrence* (flagship) - Commodore 0. H. Perry
- *Niagara* – Master Commandant Jesse D. Elliot
- *Caledonia* – Lieutenant Daniel Turner
- *Ariel* - Lieutenant John Packett
- *Trippe* - Lieutenant Joseph E. Smith
- *Tigress* - Lieutenant A. H. M. Conklin
- *Somers* - Sailing Master Thomas C. Almy
- *Scorpion* - Sailing Master Stephen Champlin
- *Ohio* - Sailing Master Daniel Dobbins
- *Porcupine* - Midshipman George Senat

Section 4

The Fleet at Put-in-Bay.

Around 10 August, the American fleet set sail to Sandusky, Ohio, at Put-in-Bay to meet with General Harrisons forces. While they were there, they supplied the ships and prepared. This is where Perry also gained 150 Kentucky riflemen; of them, 100 were sharpshooters.

While in port, many men, including Perry's brother Alexander and three fleet doctors, got lake fever. Fortunately, or due to Perry's luck, the British did not attempt to challenge him during this time.

Meanwhile, Barclay and the British were busy outfitting *Detroit* and attempting to resupply their ships. The Commander was petitioning his superiors for more men to no avail. He did not have more than 50 proper sailors for his ships; the rest were soldiers, civilian Canadians (not even militia), and Indians.

To make matters worse, there weren't enough guns to outfit his new ship, so he took them right off the ramparts of the fort to complete the ship's weapons.

Finally, he could not sit still and wanted to confront Perry and the American fleet, so he took what he had and searched for them.

Barclay Provokes The Fight

Barclay had decided he wanted a fight and immediately made it for Presque Isle. During the month of training and preparations, he had not left the view of Fort Malden, but he had gained the information of where Perry's fleet had set anchorage. He made quick time toward Put-in-Bay.

On 9 September, Perry, in the meantime, held a conference with his Captains and sharpshooters about strategy and the need to get in close and engage the British since the enemy had heavier, longer guns. That following day, the knock came to the door at Perry's cabin. Sails were seen of the British fleet outside the bay, and that next day at 7 a.m., he had the fleet ready and underway. Unfortunately, the breeze was light, so they had to tow the *Lawrence* out by small boat.

Barclay had the advantage of the wind for a time, but when the wind shifted, Perry got his men aboard, and the fleet prepared to engage the British by getting into their line of battle order. The British followed suit.

Perry Engages the British Fleet

In the Battle of Lake Erie, the Scorpion fired the initial shot at 11:45 a.m. Commodore Perry aimed to swiftly bring his flagship, the Lawrence, and the *Niagara* into carronade range. However, the light wind hindered their speed. Lawrence endured heavy fire from *Detroit* for about 20 minutes before effectively responding. Lawrence's fire fell short within the carronade range at 12:45 due to overloading the carronades. Perry fired the final shot from *Lawrence*, manning the last intact gun.

Niagara, under Elliot, was slow to engage for unknown reasons. This became a source of dispute between Perry and Elliot for years. There is conflicting witness testimony from both sides of the dispute regarding the conduct and why Elliot did not engage. Going over the whole dispute would require two separate sections of information. According to Elliott, he was following Perry's orders and staying in his position in the line of order. Others believe he was acting as a coward or possibly hoping for a quick death of Perry, perhaps even so Elliott could swoop in and save the day (There is more about this in the Appendix).

On the British side, *Queen Charlotte's* commander and First Lieutenant were killed. Lieutenant Irvine, on *Queen Charlotte*, engaged *Lawrence* closely. Despite American gunboats pounding British ships, *Lawrence* was severely damaged, with most of its crew killed or wounded. Only eighteen men were still on their feet. Expecting Perry to surrender, the British ships ceased firing, as there did not appear to be any other option.

However, Perry had other ideas. He struck down his personal flag and signaled the *Niagara* to come close. Meanwhile, the *Caledonia*, under the command of Lieutenant Daniel Turner, provided cover; Perry left *Lawrence* in a rowboat rowed by African American sailor Cyrus Tiffany, and they made their way to *Niagara* through the smoke.

The British saw the flag come down and assumed he was surrendering. However, when they finally saw his gig come out of the smoke heading toward the *Niagara*, they opened fire with every capable cannon.

Perry Transfers to Niagara. Courtesy of the Library of Congress.

Upon reaching the *Niagara*, the British gunfire stopped yet again. Perry was met at the gangway by Elliott, and Perry asked him to bring up the gunboats and gave orders. Elliott turned to and gave the orders.

As Perry assumed command of the *Niagara*, the British officers, believing they had triumphed, ordered *Lawrence's* battle flag to be lowered. However, Perry had different plans again. Despite the appearance of victory on the British side, the *Niagara* was largely unscathed, and Perry seized the opportunity to turn the tide. Hoisting his motto flag and captain's pennant, a breeze picked up, enabling Perry to maneuver swiftly.

Taking advantage of the British ships' repositioning attempt, Perry skillfully positioned the Niagara for a devastating attack. With precision, he unleashed a barrage of thirty-two-pounders and canister shots, causing havoc on the decks of the *Detroit* and *Queen Charlotte*. Simultaneously, the Niagara's rigging sharpshooters targeted the enemy, intensifying the chaos. Perry's strategic moves extended beyond the flagship duel; he directed his port gunners to disable the smaller British vessels, *Lady Prevost*, *Chippeway*, and *Little Belt*.

As the battle unfolded, Perry expertly orchestrated his assault, gradually overpowering the British fleet. *Detroit's* Captain Barclay, wounded and, recognizing the dire situation, ordered the surrender. The surrender extended to other British vessels, including *Hunter* and *Lady Prevost*, while the smaller *Chippeway* and *Little Belt* attempted to escape but were swiftly captured by American vessels. In an interesting twist of fate, *Scorpion* fired the final shot of the battle just as it had fired the first.

U.S. Brig Niagara. Courtesy of the U.S. National Park Service.

In fifteen minutes, Perry transformed an impending defeat into a decisive victory. Perry had the British captains formally surrender onboard the Lawrence deck so they could see the havoc they caused.

After the battle, Perry wrote letters to General Harrison and the Secretary of the Navy informing them of the victory and the taking of prize ships to include in the American fleet on Lake Erie.

A burial at sea was held for those who died for both sides, leaving three American and three British offices that were taken ashore at Put-in-Bay, and a funeral for them was held. Perry treated the British fairly, and Commander Barclay later commended him. Afterward, the prisoners were taken to Pittsburgh.

Procter's Retreat

Before the news of the American success on the water, General Procter was already facing a terrible situation in Amherstburg. Harrison's assaults had cut his supply lines on the land, and the busy work by Perry on the water effectively cut off the best way for those supplies to arrive. Procter had no choice but to cut his losses and abandon Amherstburg and Detroit to try and obtain supplies from somewhere else.

Chief Tecumseh disagreed and found this to be reprehensible. He argued and demanded that Procter give Fort Malden to him and his warriors to defend. Procter refused on the basis that there was no food or supplies for them. Worse yet, the armaments of the fort were taken by Barclay to outfit his ship. Tecumseh relented and was forced to join the retreat with Procter, albeit begrudgingly.

Procter's forces made their way toward Burlington Heights out to the western end of Lake Ontario.

Meanwhile, at Put-in-Bay, Perry was loaded with 2,500 soldiers to ferry them to Amherstburg after the ships were all repaired and ready. They were heading north over the water to assault and take the British base.

Along the shoreline, a mounted force of 1,000 troops led by General Richard Johnson was heading up the shore to take Detroit.

Recapture of Detroit

On 27 September, when the landing force arrived at Amherstburg, they found it abandoned. About the same day, the mounted force arrived at Detroit and was also abandoned. Both forts were taken without a shot being fired. There is little doubt that the Americans were confused at first.

It would be fair to say that both forces had figured out the direction of the retreating force. There must have been civilian witnesses still in the area the forces had questioned. Therefore, making sense that the forces made their way up the Thames River in chase of Procter and his forces, leaving on 2 October.

Battle of Thames

The combined force under General Harrison had caught up with Procter and Tecumseh's force on 4 October near Chatham, Ontario. Tecumseh and his warriors tried to slow the Americans but were quickly overwhelmed and retreated to Procter's position.

The next day at breakfast, Procter ordered his men to abandon their meals and form lines. There were no fortifications, no earthworks—nothing to slow the coming American troops. Tecumseh's warriors formed a line in the black ash swamp on the flank, hoping to catch the Americans by surprise. However, they knew they were there. Some of the men in Harrison's force were from the River Raisin, Michigan area and began to chant "Remember the River Raisin" as they approached the mixed British and Native forces.

As General Harrison surveyed the battlefield, he strategically commanded James Johnson to lead a frontal assault on the British regulars with his mounted riflemen. Despite flanking fire from Tecumseh's warriors, Johnson's Kentuckians successfully broke through, catching the British regulars off guard as their cannons remained silent. Exhausted and demoralized, the British soldiers managed only a feeble fusillade before retreating in disarray.

Following the chaos, Procter and some of his men fled the battlefield, while others, facing marshy and wooded terrain, surrendered by casting aside their weapons. Meanwhile, Tecumseh and his warriors continued to engage in fierce combat. Colonel Johnson, attempting to divert attention away from the leading American force, charged into the Indian position with a small cavalry unit. However, Tecumseh's forces responded with a deadly volley of musket fire, halting the cavalry charge and causing significant casualties. The swampy mud further hindered Johnson's advance, and it is believed that Tecumseh met his demise during this intense fighting.

As the American forces navigated through a swamp, news of Tecumseh's demise spread, leading to the dissolution of Indian resistance. While conflicting accounts credit either Richard Mentor Johnson or Revolutionary War veteran William Whitley with Tecumseh's death, it remains uncertain, leaving the possibility that both Americans may have fired on the revered Native American leader almost simultaneously.

Battle of Thames - Death of Tecumseh. Courtesy of the Library of Congress.

Perry's Promotion and Turnover of Command

Harrison and Perry, having returned to Detroit, issued a joint proclamation on 17 October 1813, announcing the cessation of armed resistance in Upper Canada. They declared that the laws and customs before the conquest were reinstated, guaranteeing the inhabitants protection under American possession. Perry, receiving a flattering letter from the Secretary of the Navy, learned of his promotion to Post Captain and was granted leave to visit his family in Rhode Island. Perry sailed with Harrison and staff on *Ariel* with nothing to detain him. En route, he stopped at Put-in-Bay, where he informed the wounded Commodore Barclay of his parole to return home.

Barclay, accompanied by his surgeon, boarded *Ariel*, who sailed for the Erie bay. Despite arriving ahead of the squadron, Perry and Harrison received a warm welcome in Erie. Avoiding demonstrations near his quarters, Perry showed considerate attention to the recovering Barclay.

Erie celebrated Perry's return in the evening, marking his first visit since building and equipping his vessels there. Perry had fulfilled his ambition, having *"met the enemy and made them his."*

Perry sailed for Black Rock the next day after a quick visit to view the remains of his old flagship in Misery Bay. Reflecting on the Battle of Lake Erie, he gave thanks for escaping unscathed amid the destruction.

On 24 October 1813, the squadron safely arrived in Black Rock, where troops were landed. Perry officially handed over command of the Erie Squadron to Jesse Elliott and, amid rejoicing, embarked on his journey east to his home in Rhode Island, bidding a final farewell to Erie. Never to return.

National Intelligencer Office,

Tuesday, September 21st, (noon.)

MOST GLORIOUS NEWS.

Copy of a letter from Com. PERRY to the Secretary of the Navy.

U. S. Brig Niagara, off the Western Sister, Head of Lake Erie, Sept. 10, 1813, 4, *P. M.*

SIR,

It has pleased the Almighty to give to the arms of the United States a signal victory over their enemies on this Lake. The British Squadron, consisting of two Ships, two Brigs, one Schooner and one Sloop, have this moment surrendered to the force under my command, after a sharp conflict.

I have the honor to be,
  Sir,
   Very Respectfully,
    Your obdt. Servant,
     O. H. PERRY.

*The hon. Wm. Jones,
Secretary of the Navy.*

SOME PARTICULARS.

Chillicothe, September 14.

Late last evening an express arrived in town from gen. Harrison's head-quar-

ters, bringing the highly gratifying intelligence of the capture of the whole of the British fleet on Lake Erie by commodore Perry. The subjoined extracts of letters from two gentlemen at headquarters, contain the most essential particulars relative to that brilliant affair.

Camp Seneca, Sept. 12:

"An express has this moment arrived from Commodore Perry, dated the 10th inst at 4 P. M. Head of Lake Erie, with the pleasing intelligence of the British fleet, consisting of two ships, two brigs and two schooners, being in our possession, with more prisoners on board than we had men to conquer them. A great many were killed on both sides"

Camp Seneca, Sept. 12.

"Victory perches on our Naval Standard! Commodore Perry has captured nearly if not all the enemy's fleet, two ships, two brigs, one sloop, and one schooner; and taken more prisoners than he had men on board."

National Intelligence Office – Perry Letter. Courtesy of the Library of Congress.

Afterward

Battle of Buffalo

Just over two months after Commodore Perry left the Erie region, The Battle of Buffalo, also known as the Battle of Black Rock, unfolded on December 30, 1813. It was a pivotal clash marked by destruction and strategic maneuvers on both sides of the Niagara River.

When Brigadier General George McClure left Fort Niagara on December 10, 1813, he decided to raze the village of Newark, which triggered a chain of events. In a swift onslaught, nearly all of Newark's 150 structures were engulfed in flames, leaving its residents with little time to flee. In response, Lieutenant General Gordon Drummond, the new Lieutenant Governor of Upper Canada, orchestrated a counteroffensive against American positions along the Niagara frontier.

Colonel John Murray's forces seized Fort Niagara in a surprise attack on December 18, while Major General Phineas Riall's troops ravaged American settlements along the lower Niagara River, decimating villages like Lewiston, Youngstown, Manchester, Tuscarora, and the military outpost of Fort Schlosser.

Drummond and Riall extended their campaign of devastation, setting their sights on the Buffalo and Black Rock villages. Crossing the Niagara under cover of darkness on December 29, Riall's forces landed near Black Rock in the early hours of December 30. While most of his men landed downstream, Lieutenant Colonel John Gordon and the Royal Scots targeted Black Rock.

Aware of the impending British assault, Major General Amos Hall rallied American forces. However, initial attempts to confront the British advance faltered, with militia units under Warren, Churchill, Adams, and Chapin fleeing at the first sign of enemy resistance.

Undeterred, Hall took command, orchestrating a defense against the British onslaught. At dawn, the air crackled with cannon and musket fire as Gordon's Royal Scots attempted to secure a foothold at Black Rock. Despite facing fierce resistance, Riall's forces pressed on, with a detachment striking the American flank.

After a valiant struggle, Hall's forces succumbed to the relentless British advance. In a bid to evade total defeat, Hall ordered a general retreat. The British pursued, descending upon Buffalo with ferocity. The village was pillaged and razed, with only a handful of buildings spared the flames.

The devastation extended beyond the villages. Riall's troops laid waste to the navy yard, and several vessels, including four American ships, docked there, the *Chippeway*, *Ariel*, *Little Belt*, and *Trippe*. Black Rock and the town of Buffalo, except for one building, was reduced to ash before the British withdrew, crossing the Niagara back into Canadian territory.

Burning of Buffalo. Courtesy of New York Public Library.

Perry and Elliot Public Feud

Shortly after the Battle of Lake Erie, there were heated exchanges between the crew members regarding the conduct of Jesse Elliot while in command of the *Niagara*.

One side of the feud claimed Elliot was a coward and refused to engage in the battle, possibly hoping Perry would die that day. The other side maintained that he acted per his orders and with honor.

The feud eventually broke out between the two commanders openly to the point that they and their supportive crew members quarreled over it. It was so widespread that even the British Commanders were writing letters in support of or against the actions of that day.

Turner Captured at Thames River.

In the summer of 1814, Daniel Turner transferred from the *Caledonia* to command the schooner *Scorpion*, a vessel that would soon become synonymous with daring exploits on Lakes Erie and Huron. Assigned to support army operations around Detroit, Turner played a crucial role in blockading British forces at the Nottawasaga River and Lake Simcoe. His leadership came to the forefront in July 1814 when he, under the command of Arthur Sinclair, executed a hit-and-run raid at St. Mary River in Upper Canada. The raid captured a small merchantman, the Mink, marking a strategic victory for the American forces.

Following the success at St. Mary River, Sinclair extended the reach of their operation by dispatching Turner with a detachment of seamen and regulars led by Andrew Holmes to venture deeper into enemy territory. Turner's mission involved destroying enemy buildings and possessions, coupled with the fiery demise of an enemy schooner. Despite the challenges, Turner returned victorious to American territory in Michilimackinac (Fort Mackinac), reuniting with Sinclair.

However, the tides turned on September 6, 1814, when Turner and his command faced an unexpected setback. While bringing the *Scorpion* alongside the former American schooner *Tigress*, Turner was unaware that the *Tigress* had fallen into British hands a few days earlier. In a twist of fate, the British captured Turner and his crew.

The Capture of Scorpion. Courtesy of the U.S. Naval Institute.

Turner was imprisoned at the now-retaken British Fort Mackinac, only to return to the United States in exchange for a British prisoner of war. He was sent to Rhode Island to meet and serve again under his former commander, Commodore Perry.

Perry's Command of USS Java

In May 1814, Perry commanded a squadron of gunboats at Providence, Rhode Island. This did not last long, as two months later, he was assigned to command the new ship, *USS Java*, a 44-gun frigate that was being outfitted.

At the same time, the British attacked Baltimore and Washington, DC. Perry was tasked to assist in the defense and then turned to the same when the British invaded Chesapeake Bay. Not long after, the fighting came to an end, and the Treaty of Ghent was signed, bringing an end to the War of 1812. The *USS Java* was not entirely completed in outfitting.

At the end of the fighting, Perry had received orders for his Second-in-Command, Lieutenant Daniel Turner. Together, they finished preparing the ship to get underway, and the ship left Baltimore Shipyard on August 5, 1815, heading to Hampton Roads, New York, then Newport, Rhode Island, for gear and crew before setting out to the Mediterranean to serve in the Second Barbary War.

The Battle of New Orleans

The Battle of New Orleans, on January 8, 1815, was a significant victory for the United States against Great Britain during the War of 1812, marking the conflict's final major battle. Despite a peace treaty signed in Ghent, Belgium, a few weeks earlier, both British and American troops were unaware and clashed in New Orleans.

In autumn 1814, a British fleet led by Gen. Edward Pakenham aimed to seize New Orleans, strategically located at the mouth of the Mississippi River, with hopes of expanding into U.S. territory acquired through the Louisiana Purchase. Gen. Andrew Jackson swiftly defended the city upon hearing of the British presence.

Jackson declared martial law and organized defenses, including enlisting various groups like aristocrats, freed slaves, and Native Americans, totaling over 4,000. Defensive structures, notably "Line Jackson," were erected using logs, earth, and cotton bales.

The battle occurred outside New Orleans, with American forces split into defensive positions on both banks of the Mississippi. Jackson led the defense on the eastern bank, while Gen. David Morgan commanded the western bank of 1,000 soldiers.

The Battle of New Orleans. Courtesy of Library of Congress

On January 8, 1815, about 8,000 British soldiers, led by Pakenham, launched a full-scale attack but suffered heavy casualties, including Pakenham himself. Gen. John Lambert took command but ultimately withdrew. The battle lasted about two hours, resulting in significant British casualties. Despite their smaller numbers, the Americans injured around 2,000 British soldiers while sustaining fewer than 65 casualties themselves.

Although the battle didn't impact the war's outcome, it bolstered Jackson's reputation, helping him secure the presidency in 1828.

Epilogue

Epilogue

The Effects of the War of 1812

The War of 1812 profoundly impacted American and British histories, shaping the trajectory of nations and sparking significant geopolitical shifts. Despite ending in a draw on the battlefield, the conflict ultimately reshaped the political and cultural landscapes on both sides of the Atlantic.

The Treaty of Ghent, signed in 1814, ushered in an era of restoration as both the United States and Britain agreed to revert to the pre-war status quo. While neither side could claim outright victory, the war solidified America's position as a formidable player on the international stage. The resilience displayed in facing off against the world's preeminent military power bolstered American nationalism and garnered respect from the global community.

For the United States, the aftermath of the War of 1812 marked a period of burgeoning nationalism and diplomatic assertion. The Monroe Doctrine, articulated during James Monroe's presidency, asserted American influence in the Western Hemisphere and set the tone for future foreign policy endeavors. This era, aptly termed the "Era of Good Feeling," witnessed a surge in patriotic sentiment and confidence in the nation's abilities. Conversely, the War of 1812 spelled the demise of the Federalist Party in America. With their opposition to the conflict, Federalists found themselves marginalized in the political landscape, paving the way for the dominance of other parties and ideologies.

However, amidst the victories and political realignments, the War of 1812 exacted a heavy toll on indigenous nations in North America. Wars such as Tecumseh's War in the Old Northwest and the Creek War in the Old Southwest defeated these peoples, opening the door for westward expansion and threatening their traditional ways of life east of the Mississippi River. The conflict fueled the forces of territorial expansion, posing existential challenges to indigenous communities and their sovereignty.

Meanwhile, across the Atlantic, the war's impact was felt in the survival of British colonies in Canada. The British victory in defending Canada solidified its position and laid the groundwork for the Canadian Confederation. Had the War of 1812 not occurred, historians speculate that Canada may have become part of the United States due to significant migration patterns.

In essence, the War of 1812 catalyzed a period of transformation, leaving enduring legacies that reverberated through the corridors of power and the lives of marginalized communities. Its echoes resonate in diplomatic doctrines, political realignments, and the struggles of indigenous peoples, underscoring the complexities and consequences of historical conflict.

The Second Barbary War

During the Second Barbary War, which followed the War of 1812 and was initiated by President Madison's call for action against Algiers (who supported Britain during the War of 1812), the United States, led by Commodore Decatur, aimed to tackle Algerian piracy against American shipping. Decatur's successful battles, resulting in the capture of Meshouda and the death of corsair Raïs Hamidou, led to a peace deal in late 1815. This agreement ended tribute payments, granted full shipping rights, and freed enslaved Americans of the merchant vessel *Edwin*.

While the defeat of Algiers in 1815 weakened Barbary pirate dominance, the U.S. remained cautious due to historical treaty violations by the Barbary nations. 1816 President Madison deployed Commodore Isaac Chauncey's squadron to protect American interests when Algerians threatened the peace treaty. Additionally, a Dutch and British fleet forced Algiers to release over 1,000 European slaves.

Despite initial victories and diplomatic efforts, the Barbary States' piracy persisted, prompting continued international pressure. While some European nations continued paying tribute, the U.S. took a firm stance. Though there were punitive measures like British bombardments, lasting peace only came with the French conquest of Algeria in 1830.

The Presidency of Willian Henry Harrison

William Harrison resigned from the Army in 1814 and returned to Ohio, later facing financial struggles that led him back into politics. He was elected to the House of Representatives in 1816 and served in the Senate from 1819 to 1821. In 1828, he became Minister Plenipotentiary (a junior-level Ambassador) to Colombia, but he quickly became critical of the country's leadership, describing it as on the brink of anarchy. Harrison's denunciations led to his recall by President Jackson in 1829 at Colombia's request.

Returning to the United States, Harrison lived a relatively modest life on his farm, relying on savings, a small pension, and farm income. Despite financial challenges, he remained active in local affairs, serving on the vestry of Christ Church and later as Clerk of Courts for Hamilton County. He also engaged in agricultural pursuits, including farming and whiskey production, although he eventually regretted his involvement in the liquor industry.

Harrison's encounter with abolitionist George DeBaptiste led to a friendship and highlighted his evolving views on slavery. He distanced himself from alcohol production and expressed hope for a future without slavery in North America. Despite financial struggles, Harrison remained respected by many, as demonstrated by a grand reception in Philadelphia in 1836, indicative of his popularity among Pennsylvanians who fought alongside him.

Harrison's political ambitions continued, culminating in his candidacy for president in 1836 and 1840 as a Whig nominee. His campaigns capitalized on his military background, contrasting with the economic challenges under the incumbent Van Buren. Utilizing symbols like the log cabin and hard cider, Harrison portrayed himself as a man of the people, contrasting with the elitist image attributed to Van Buren.

The 1840 election saw a high turnout, with Harrison winning a landslide victory in the Electoral College. His campaign slogan, "Tippecanoe and Tyler, Too," and his reputation as the hero of the Battle of Tippecanoe contributed to his success. Despite criticism from opponents, Harrison's populist appeal and portrayal as a humble frontiersman resonated with voters, which led to his triumph over Van Buren.

President William H. Harrison. Courtesy of The Smithsonian Institute.

He became the ninth President of the United States and became ill shortly after his inauguration. Then, on his 32nd day, he became the first President to die in office and earned the status of serving the shortest tenure in U.S. Presidential history.

The Death of Oliver Perry

Commodore Oliver Perry was entrusted with the command of the *USS Java* in 1815 and tasked with addressing the ongoing challenges of the Barbary pirates in the Mediterranean. However, an unfortunate altercation during their stay in Naples led to Perry slapping *Java's* Marine officer, John Heath. Perry and Heath faced court-martial and were found guilty, though they received lenient reprimands. Subsequently, Heath challenged Perry to a duel, which took place on October 19, 1817. Despite the duel being held at the infamous site of

Aaron Burr's fatal encounter with Alexander Hamilton, Perry, showing restraint, refused to fire after Heath's initial shot missed.

During this tumultuous period, Perry was entangled in another conflict, this time with Jesse Duncan Elliott, regarding the actions at the Battle of Lake Erie. Elliott challenged Perry to a duel following a series of heated exchanges. Still, Perry refused and opted to settle the matter through formal court-martial charges against Elliott, aiming to end the discord. However, the Secretary of the Navy, concerned about potential scandal and division among officers, passed the decision to President James Monroe, who chose to suppress the issue, closing the chapter on the Perry-Elliott controversy.

To divert Perry's attention from these confrontations, President Monroe appointed him to lead a diplomatic mission to South America in June 1819. Perry embarked on the *USS John Adams*, later transferring to the Nonsuch to navigate the Orinoco River to Angostura, Venezuela. Despite the prevalence of yellow fever in the region, Perry managed to maintain his health. Still, twenty crewmen aboard the *Nonsuch* succumbed to the illness, emphasizing the dangers of the mission.

Having completed his diplomatic objectives, Perry set sail back to Trinidad, where tragedy struck. On August 15, 1819, Perry fell ill with yellow fever, and despite valiant efforts by the crew to reach port, he passed away on August 23, 1819, his 34th birthday, marking the untimely end of a distinguished naval career.

The Command of Daniel Turner

Daniel Turner embarked on a distinguished naval career that spanned various significant assignments and showcased his leadership prowess. Commencing his journey as a Midshipman aboard the *USS Constitution*, Turner's dedication and skill propelled him to eventually assume command of the same vessel, a testament to his rise through the ranks.

After Lake Erie, from 1815 to 1817, Turner served as second-in-command on the frigate *Java* under the leadership of his former superior, Oliver Hazard Perry. The deployment in the Mediterranean included strategic visits to Algiers and Tripoli, demonstrating American naval strength and dissuading Barbary pirates from violating treaties with the United States. After this mission, *Java* returned to Newport, Rhode Island, where the vessel was laid up.

Between 1819 and 1824, Turner navigated the seas as Commander of the schooner *Nonsuch*, once again under the leadership of Oliver Hazard Perry. This period saw him suppressing West Indian piracy and participating in a diplomatic mission up the Orinoco River to Venezuela. Tragically, during this assignment, his mentor, Perry, succumbed to yellow fever, leaving Turner to navigate the ship through challenging circumstances. The subsequent years on the *Nonsuch* involved patrolling the U.S. East Coast, combating piracy in the West Indies, and a brief Mediterranean cruise in 1824.

In 1826, Turner, along with Daniel Dobbins, undertook the solemn duty of returning to Brazil to retrieve the body of Commodore Oliver Perry, marking a poignant chapter in Turner's career. Following shore duty in Boston, Massachusetts, he assumed command of the *USS Erie* in 1827 as part of the West Indies Squadron.

Turner's leadership skills led to his promotion to Captain in 1835, culminating in his command of the *USS Constitution* in 1839, where he navigated the Pacific Squadron until his relief in 1841. From 1843 to 1846, Turner commanded the American squadron along the Brazilian coast, followed by a role as Commandant at the Portsmouth Navy Yard, showcasing his versatility and commitment to naval service.

The Legacy of Daniel Dobbins

Daniel Dobbins, a distinguished figure in maritime history, emerged as a critical player following his service during the War of 1812. His strategic navigation skills and influential advocacy profoundly impacted the maritime domain, leaving a legacy far beyond his naval service.

During the War of 1812, Dobbins's pivotal role in facilitating the transportation of vital supplies to Detroit aboard the schooner *Ohio* demonstrated his unwavering dedication to supporting ground offensives. Post-war, his contributions continued as he partnered with Colonel John Miller in 1816 to chart the waters of Green Bay and establish a fort, further aiding safe water commissions.

Transitioning from his naval career in 1826, Dobbins embarked on a new phase marked by advocacy and leadership within the Revenue Cutter Service, the precursor to the United States Coast Guard. Notably, his lobbying efforts led to establishing a United States Revenue Cutter Service station in Erie. Appointed as commander of the *USRC Benjamin Rush* in 1829 by President Andrew Jackson, Dobbins's leadership was pivotal. However, his political affiliations occasionally intersected with his military responsibilities, causing fluctuations in his command positions.

Despite facing temporary reassignments due to political shifts, Dobbins's commitment to duty remained steadfast. His eventual return to the *USRC Erie* in 1847 underscored his enduring connection to the region and maritime interests.

Captain Dobbins's passing in Erie on February 29, 1856, marked the end of a remarkable career characterized by service and dedication. His enduring contributions to maritime safety and security are reflected in the Coast Guard station in Erie, serving as a testament to his lasting impact. Today, Dobbins rests in peace at the Erie Cemetery, remembered for his significant role in shaping maritime history.

The American Captains

Oliver Hazard Perry (Lawrence)

Much has already been written about the life and career of the Commodore, including what is written in this book. Therefore, I won't go into too much detail now. Here is what I will say. He was the oldest of five sons, all of whom served in the Navy, one of them being Mathew C. Perry, who commanded the Perry Expedition that ended Japanese Isolationism. Oliver also had three sisters; one never married, another married a Commodore, and the third married a Congressman.

Outside the Navy, Oliver and his wife had five children, four growing up 'to maturity.' The second of five children, named Oliver H Perry II, passed away after thirteen months of age. The remaining children were three boys and a girl. All three boys served in the military, and his daughter married Reverend Francis Vinton.

As I stated in the introduction of this work, Oliver passed away on his birthday at the age of thirty-four; he was at sea. He is buried in Newport, Rhode Island.

Jesse Duncan Elliot (Niagara)

Jesse Elliot, born in Maryland in 1782, overcame early tragedy after his father died in an Indian attack to pursue a career marked by naval service and controversy. Joining the United States Navy as a midshipman in 1804, Elliot rose through the ranks, demonstrating valor during the War of 1812, notably in the Battle of Lake Erie. However, his relationship with his superior, Oliver Perry, soured, leading to a duel challenge and a court-martial. Despite accolades from Congress and Perry's commendation, Elliot's contentious nature and political affiliations, particularly with the Jacksonian faction, ensured his legacy would remain clouded by controversy.

Controversy followed Elliot throughout his naval career, including his command of the West Indies Squadron and tenure as Commandant of the Boston Naval Yard. Notably, his decision to mount a figurehead of Andrew Jackson on the *U.S.S. Constitution* sparked outrage in the Whig-leaning city of Boston. Later, while leading the Mediterranean Squadron, Elliot faced criticism for accepting gifts from foreign representatives, culminating in a court-martial and suspension from the Navy for four years. He was returned to duty in October 1843 by order of the President and assigned to Philadelphia Naval Yard.

Despite setbacks, Elliot's dedication to naval service endured until he died in 1845. His son, Washington Lafayette Elliot, following in his father's footsteps, pursued a distinguished career in the Army. Jesse Elliot's complex legacy reflects his contributions to American naval history and the controversies that shadowed his path.

Daniel Turner (Caledonia)

Daniel Turner was born in 1794 and joined the Navy as a midshipman in 1808. Turner swiftly rose through the ranks, displaying remarkable leadership and bravery throughout his career. Notable among his assignments was his command of the brig Niagara during the Battle of Lake Erie in 1813, where his strategic maneuvers significantly contributed to the American victory. Turner's gallantry in this battle earned him accolades, including praise from Oliver Hazard Perry, a Congressional medal, and a sword from the state of New York.

Following his heroic exploits on Lake Erie, Turner continued his naval service with dedication and distinction. He commanded various vessels, including the schooner *Scorpion*, engaging in crucial operations during the War of 1812, such as blockading British forces and conducting raids. Turner's leadership and tactical acumen were further showcased during his deployments in the Mediterranean, where he served under Perry in the frigate *Java*, demonstrating American naval strength to the Barbary pirates. His commitment to duty persisted throughout his career, whether combating piracy in the West Indies or commanding the American squadron along the Brazilian coast.

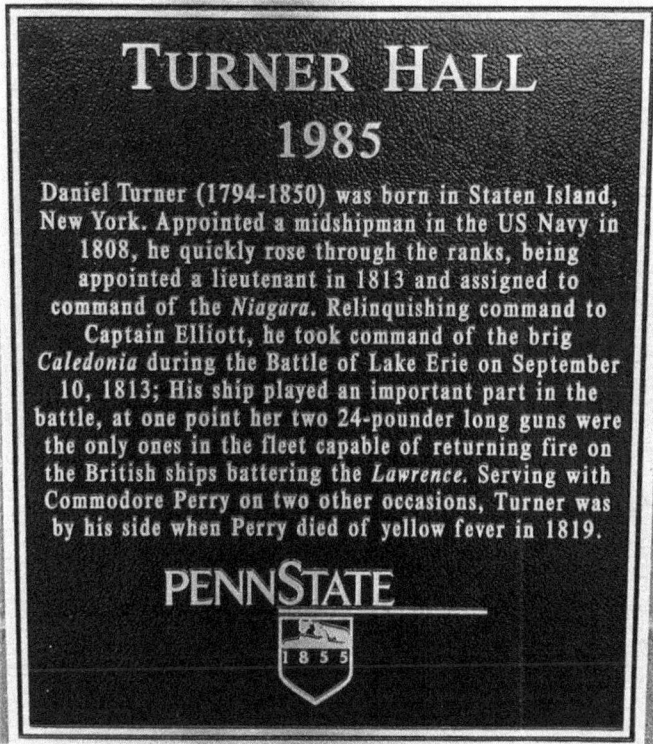

Turner Hall Marker at Pennsylvania State University. Courtesy of The Historical Marker Database.

Promoted to Captain in 1835, Turner's illustrious career set him on the path to commanding renowned ships like the *USS Constitution* and leading vital missions across different naval theaters. Despite facing periods of shore duty, Turner's passion for maritime service remained undiminished. His final assignment as Commandant of the Portsmouth Navy Yard reflected his enduring dedication to naval operations. Turner's sudden passing in 1850 marked the end of a remarkable career and left a legacy of valor, leadership, and unwavering commitment to the United States Navy.

Thomas Holdup Stevens (Trippe)

Thomas Holdup Stevens, born in 1795 in Charleston, South Carolina, became an orphan early but found support and mentorship from figures like Colonel Daniel Stevens and Navy Lieutenant Ralph DeLancy Izard. Adopting the surname Stevens in 1815, he embarked on a distinguished naval career, showcasing bravery during the War of 1812. Notably, in 1813, he served under Oliver Hazard Perry at Erie, commanding the sloop Trippe in the Battle of Lake Erie and receiving accolades despite not being specifically

Thomas Holdup Stevens. Courtesy of NavSource.

mentioned in dispatches, which were attributed to differences with superiors.

Following the war, Stevens continued to excel in various naval assignments, demonstrating leadership and valor. He consistently displayed gallantry and professionalism, from combating pirates in the West Indies to commanding ships in the Mediterranean Squadron. Recognized for his contributions, he rose through the ranks, eventually becoming Captain and overseeing the Washington Navy Yard before his untimely death in 1841.

Described as the epitome of chivalry and possessing literary talent, Stevens left a lasting legacy not only in his naval service but also in his family life, leaving behind descendants who continued his honorable name and memory. His miniature portrait, depicting a man of solid features and scarred cheek, symbolizes his enduring spirit and commitment to duty. Buried initially in the Congressional Cemetery, he was moved to his final resting place at Arlington National Cemetery to honor his service to the nation.

Stephen Champlin (Scorpion)

Steven Champlin, a distinguished naval officer born on November 17, 1789, in South Kingston, Rhode Island, and passing away on February 20, 1870, in Buffalo, New York, had a remarkable career that began with humble origins and culminated in significant contributions to American naval history. Despite receiving a common-school education only, Champlin's ambition led him to the sea at sixteen, quickly rising to captain a brig in the West India trade by twenty-two. His naval career officially commenced on May 22, 1812, when he was appointed a Sailing Master in the United States Navy, demonstrating exceptional ability and promptness in his duties.

Stephen Champlin. Courtesy of Buffalo Historical Society.

In July 1813, Champlin was tasked with a daring mission, leading a group across Lakes Ontario and Erie to report to Commodore Perry in Erie, Pennsylvania. He displayed remarkable resilience and skill and completed the arduous journey in just five days. His bravery shone during the Battle of Lake Erie on September 10, 1813, where he commanded the *Scorpion*, playing a pivotal role in capturing enemy vessels despite being under twenty-four years old.

Champlin's valor continued as he commanded various vessels and engaged in strategic blockades, notably at Mackinac in 1814. However, his career faced a setback when he was severely wounded and captured by British and Indian forces. Despite enduring prolonged suffering, he persevered, eventually retiring to Connecticut due to his injuries, though he briefly served on the receiving ship Fulton from 1828 to 1834 before relocating to Buffalo.

Despite his physical limitations, Champlin's dedication to the Navy remained unwavering. He ascended through the ranks, achieving the rank of Commodore in 1862, and became the last survivor of the Battle of Lake Erie.

His legacy as a courageous and dedicated naval officer endures, reflecting his significant contributions to American maritime history.

John H. Packet (Ariel)

At around 23 years old, Lieutenant John Packet, with just six weeks in grade, possessed rare ship-to-ship combat experience as the commanding officer of the schooner *Ariel*. Despite being described in his 1815 efficiency report as lacking in professional expertise and industry, Packet had served as a midshipman on the Constitution during two significant battles, making him a valuable asset during wartime engagements.

A Virginia native, he began his naval career as a midshipman in 1809 and swiftly rose to Lieutenant shortly before the referenced battle. His involvement in capturing *HMS Java* under Bainbridge's command showcased his early prowess. Despite his achievements, Packet's life was cut short by fever while serving at Erie following the battle, as detailed in Benson J Lossing's 'Pictorial Field Book of the War of 1812.'

Tragically, his promising career was cut short by illness, although he left a legacy of bravery and dedication to his service.

Augustus H. M. Conklin (Somers)

Augustus H. M. Conklin, a Virginia native, served as a midshipman from 1809 and rose to Lieutenant by 1813. In 1814, Conklin's vessel was captured off Fort Erie by a party in boats at night. Despite his promising career, he left the Navy in 1820 while stationed at Portsmouth, New Hampshire.

Thomas C. Almy (Tigress)

Thomas C. Almy (1787-1813), a Quaker from Rhode Island, commenced his naval journey in his youth, showcasing remarkable skills that led to his first command at just twenty-one. Notably, during the pivotal Battle of Lake Erie on September 10, 1813, Almy demonstrated adept leadership as the commanding officer of the schooner *Somers*, deftly maneuvering his vessel to engage the smaller British fleet.

Tragically, after the battle fell victim to pneumonia, passing away in December 1813, still in Erie. In recognition of his valor, Almy was posthumously honored with a commemorative engraved sword, given to his family as a testament to his contributions during the Battle of Lake Erie.

George Senat (Porcupine)

In his book, Benson Lossing recounts the life of George Senat as a New Orleans native of French descent. Senat began his career as a sailor, though details of his early life remain unknown. After the Battle of Lake Erie, he continued to serve on the upper lakes in 1814 before returning to Erie, where he got into a dispute with Sailing Master McDonald, resulting in a fatal duel for Senat at the corner of what is now Third and Sassafras Streets.

The British Captains

Robert Heriot Barclay (Detroit)

Robert Heriot Barclay, born in Kettle, Scotland 1786, commenced his naval journey at 11, embarking on the ship Anson as a midshipman. His career soared as he joined Lord Nelson's *Victory* and later proved his mettle as a Lieutenant during the Battle of Trafalgar in 1805, notably rescuing sailors from the sinking Redoubtable. Barclay's valor and expertise shone further in command of the *Diana*, although he suffered the loss of an arm in a daring encounter with a French convoy in 1809.

Commodore Robert Barclay. Courtesy of Naval , History and Heritage Command.

Transferred to North America, Barclay awaited a promotion that never came, instead becoming thrust into the action of the War of 1812, facing off against Captain Oliver Hazard Perry. Despite Perry's advantages in resources, Barclay courageously led his forces, only to be defeated at the Battle of Lake Erie in 1813, surrendering the British fleet to Perry. Remarkably, Barclay's conduct in defeat earned him admiration, as he was acquitted by a court-martial that praised his gallantry and judgment. He was finally promoted to Commander in November of 1814.

Beyond the battlefield, Barclay's personal life grew as he married Agnes Cosser in 1815, with whom he had several children. However, his post-war years were marked by frustration as he struggled to secure another naval command. He received only a minor appointment to a bomb vessel in 1822 that lasted only two years. Until he died in 1837, it appears that he was no longer in service. Despite this, Barclay's legacy endures through his bravery in battle, immortalizing him as a distinguished figure in naval history.

Robert Finnis (Queen Charlotte)

Captain Robert Finnis, a native of Kent, England, born in 1784, tragically met his end on September 10, 1813, after sixteen years of service to the Royal Navy. Joining the Royal Navy as a Midshipman in 1797, he distinguished himself early on. He commanded a boat during the daring raid to capture the French Corvette *La Chevrette* in Camaret Bay on July 21, 1801, earning a promotion to Lieutenant for his bravery.

At the onset of the War of 1812, he was assigned to *Queen Charlotte* on Lake Erie, where he made the ultimate sacrifice in his line of duty during the pivotal Battle of Lake Erie.

A memorial for Captain Finnis is erected at St Leonard Church in Kent, England.

Edward Wise Buchan (Lady Prevost)

His first known dates of service in the Royal Navy began in November 1800, later earning an appointment as Lieutenant aboard *HMS Inconstant* in November 1803.

He married Mary Robertson in April 1808, with whom he had at least one child named William, born in 1810.

Transferred to Canada at the onset of the War of 1812, he assumed command of the Lady Prevost, playing a pivotal role as its Commander in the Battle of Lake Erie. Tragically, he sustained mortal wounds during the battle and passed away on 22 Feb 1814 as a result of his injuries sustained in the conflict.

John F. Breman (Little Belt)

Efforts to uncover details about the life and career of Lieutenant Breman have yielded little insight into his origins or ultimate fate despite thorough searches across various resources. Commander Barclay's sparse mention of Breman or the *Little Belt* following the surrender during his reports on the Battle of Lake Erie has made me curious about Barclay's views on Breman's actions. While it is uncertain why Breman's role is underplayed, this lack of information may encourage further inquiry into the circumstances surrounding his involvement.

While researching John Breman, additional documentation and scenarios touching upon espionage and sabotage were referenced, although not directly. I do not want to speculate, nor am I making an assertion here regarding Breman's involvement in such activities. Nonetheless, it would be prudent for both readers and fellow researchers to acknowledge the potential significance of these references and either explore them further or dismiss them accordingly.

George Bignell (General Hunter)

George Bignell, born on December 1, 1786, came from a distinguished naval lineage, a veteran Purser of the Royal Navy, the son of John Bignell. Additionally, he was related to notable figures in the Navy, including Commander E. H. Kenney and Dr. James Anderson, Deputy Medical Inspector of Hasler Hospital. Bignell commenced his naval career as a Midshipman in June 1795 aboard the *Andromeda* under Captain William Taylor.

In March 1801, Bignell was appointed Acting Lieutenant on the *London* under Captain Robert Waller Otway and participated in the decisive battle of Copenhagen on April 2. He continued his service aboard the London until the peace, subsequently serving on several other ships, including the *Spartiate* under Captain Sir Erasmus Laforey, with whom he fought at Trafalgar. Bignell's naval service extended to guarding the coast of Sicily, landing troops in the Bay of Naples, and participating in reducing the islands of Ischia and Procida.

Bignell's bravery and dedication to duty were further demonstrated when, in command of *General Hunter*, he engaged in a fierce battle with a superior American force on Lake Erie under Commodore Perry in September 1813. Severely wounded and taken prisoner, Bignell endured captivity until July 1814. Despite his hardships, he attained the rank of Commander on September 19, 1815, a testament to his valor and leadership on the battlefield.

Bignell retired from active duty on February 16, 1816, and married Charlotte Patchon on May 25, 1816, and they had six children together. Though his naval career concluded, Commander Bignell's legacy remains one of unwavering courage, steadfast loyalty, and exemplary service to the Royal Navy.

John Campbell (Chippeway)

To the best of my ability, I could not find anything more about John Campbell's life before the Battle of Lake Erie. His Commander Barclay lists him as slightly wounded in his report to his seniors after the battle, but nothing else is mentioned.

I searched the genealogy databases using his name, career, and known place at the battle and found that two John Campbells were released after the war. One was born in 1787, and the other was born in 1780. Both have a wife, and both list their occupation as a Cooper. However, this does not mean that either of these men was Master's Mate Campbell.

Appendix

Endnotes

The Dispute Between Perry and Elliott

A prolonged and intense feud between Oliver H. Perry and Jesse Elliott lasted for over three decades regarding Elliott's actions during the Battle of Lake Erie. Elliott maintained that he adhered strictly to Perry's battle plan, refusing to advance his position to assist Perry's beleaguered ship, the Lawrence. However, Perry did not publicly criticize Elliott, and discussions about his lack of action circulated among naval officers on both sides. Despite receiving a public statement from Perry affirming his correct conduct, Elliott spent the rest of his life attempting to tarnish Perry's reputation, even challenging Perry to a duel, which Perry declined.

Perry contemplated formal charges against Elliott in 1818 but was advised against it by the Secretary of the Navy. Perry had accused Elliott of failing to provide timely support. At the same time, Elliott argued that Perry's lack of communication and signals contributed to the confusion. The controversy over their actions at the Battle of Lake Erie persisted even after the death of Perry in 1819.

Leaving behind a list of accusations with Commodore Stephen Decatur before departing on a diplomatic mission, Perry's charges resurfaced years later when Decatur was killed in a duel in which Elliott acted as a second. Decatur's widow subsequently published Perry's charges, holding Elliott partly accountable for her husband's death, further fueling the bitter feud between the two naval officers.

The USS Constitution Volunteers

Events within the lake theater were not the only influence that led to victory at the Battle of Lake Erie; there were also developments in Boston, Massachusetts. The British blockade outside Boston in 1813 played a pivotal role in reshaping the composition and effectiveness of the United States Navy away from the coast. With the *USS Constitution* temporarily sidelined in Boston Harbor, seasoned sailors were redirected to support operations in the Great Lakes region, including Lake Erie (and Lake Champlain).

The success of the *Constitution* had bolstered national morale, prompting the transfer of experienced crew members to where they were needed. These veterans brought crucial expertise to a relatively inexperienced naval force, contributing to the pivotal outcome of the battle. Despite initial challenges and the unpopularity of lake duty among sailors, the infusion of seasoned personnel from the *Constitution* proved instrumental in shaping the course of the War of 1812.

Commodore Oliver Hazard Perry faced significant constraints due to the lack of seasoned sailors within his ranks. His crew, described as diverse and inexperienced, posed a challenge to the ambitious objectives set for the naval operations on the lake. However, Perry's aspirations were bolstered by the arrival of veteran crew members from the *Constitution*, enhancing the capabilities and morale of the Lake Erie squadron. Despite the less prestigious nature of lake duty compared to maritime assignments, the transfer of experienced personnel signaled a strategic shift in utilizing resources to achieve crucial victories in the ongoing conflict.

The infusion of expertise and winning mentality from the *Constitution* veterans proved decisive in tipping the balance in favor of the American fleet during the Battle of Lake Erie, underscoring the significance of strategic resource allocation and personnel management in naval warfare during the War of 1812.

Battle flag of Oliver Perry.

Oliver Hazard Perry's famous rallying cry, "Don't give up the ship!" originated from the dying words of Captain James Lawrence, spoken after he was wounded aboard the Chesapeake in 1813. Perry, deeply moved by Lawrence's bravery, named his flagship in honor of him and adopted the phrase as a symbol of resilience.

Perry wanted a battle flag to accompany this ship and turned to Margaret Forster Steuart. She was the wife of Army Captain Thomas Steuart and sister

106

to Thomas Forster, both friends of Perry's. Forster was the commander of the Erie Light Infantry that had guarded the fleet. Steuart, her sister Dorcas, and five of her nieces handcrafted the flag quickly in a few days, embodying Perry's determination and the spirit of Lawrence's words.

Perry's flag, bearing the immortal words of Captain Lawrence, endures as a symbol of unwavering resolve and patriotism and is on at the US Naval Academy Museum in Annapolis, Maryland, and serves as a poignant reminder of naval history and the enduring motto of the US Navy.

Index

References and Resources

In my research, I read a lot of sources. The following list is just a portion of them, but the ones that I recommend the most for those who follow behind me or are interested in following up on some of the information I have presented in this book.

I encourage you to take the time to look them over and any other sources you find out there.

Books

The Lake Erie Campaign of 1813 by Walter P. Rybka.

Signal Victory by David C. Skaggs and Gerard T. Altoff.

History of the Battle of Lake Erie by William W. Dobbins.

Pictorial Field Book of the War of 1812 by Benson J. Lossing.

Website Articles

NPS. 2023, The Battle of Lake Erie, National Park Service. September 30, 2023.
https://www.nps.gov/pevi/learn/historyculture/battle_erie_detail.htm

Heidler, David & Jeanne. 2024. War of 1812, Britannica. January 2024. https://www.britannica.com/event/War-of-1812

Websites

American Battlefield Trust: https://www.battlefields.org/

The USS Constitution Museum: https://ussconstitutionmuseum.org/

U.S. Naval Institute: https://www.usni.org/

The Canadian Encyclopedia:
https://www.thecanadianencyclopedia.ca/en

Locations

The Erie Maritime Museum
150 E Front Street
Erie, PA 16507

https://www.eriemaritimemuseum.org/

About the Author

Jason Albers is a historian, researcher, and author passionate about family history, maritime tales, and religious studies. He is married and has adult children he keeps in touch with as often as possible.

His journey began at eleven when he became a certified scuba diver, setting the stage for a lifetime of adventures worldwide. His adventures continued into adulthood, where he served in the United States Navy and the Army National Guard.

Extending his real-world experiences with academic pursuits, Jason earned an undergraduate degree in Security Management while working as a private investigator. He later achieved a Doctorate in Religious Studies, emphasizing history and archaeology.

Jason intends to explore religion's influence on global maritime cultures throughout history. Beyond that, he enjoys unraveling the stories behind his family tree and others. No matter what discoveries lie ahead, he looks forward to the journeys.

Oliver Perry Monument. Courtesy of Jason Albers.